THE SMOOTHIES & JUICE MAKER RECIPE BOOK

Delicious recipes for smoothies for weight loss, good health and energy

Dr. Erick Mackarni

Table of content

Fruity Almond Sip

Banana Spiced Oatmeal

Vanilla Berry Surprise

Slimming Citrus Swirl

Rich Tropicana Pine

Watermelon Fruit Fiddle

WEIGHT LOSS SMOOTHIES

Citrus Carrot Flakes

Beet Breeze Trim

Cherry Tomato Surprise

Spinach Apple Burner

Fruity Kale Splash

Creamy Apple & Blueberry

Mixed Apple Energy

Strawberry Pear Sherbet Blueberry

Pineapple Custard

Papaya & Kale Sunset

Cool Green Garden

Mixed Fruit Spinach

GREEN SMOOTHIES

Zesty Avocado Mango

Spinach Berry Refresh

Mixed Greens Pineapple

Kale Banana Mist

Kiwi Pear Crush

Mint Mango Summer

Celery Wonder Punch

Pineapple Spinach Splash

Mixed Apple Jubilee

Green Ginger Candy

HIGH ENERGY & PROTEIN RICH SMOOTHIES

Apple Vanilla Crunch

Nutty Spiced Banana

Cherry Blueberry Jiggle

Citrus Banana Zest

Gingery Papaya Power

Mango Nilla Fudge

Chocolaty Almond Banza

Strawberry Chocolate Medal

Pistachio Mango Cream

Blueberry Chia Delight

LOW SUGAR & DIABETIC SMOOTHIES

Kiwi Peach Sorbet

Dandelion Greens Shimmer

Strawberry Pixie

Apple Almond Pearl

Cranapple Green Pie

Papaya Green Sauce

Spinach Cherry Blossom

Cantaloupe Swizzle

Gingery Peach Boogie

Blackberry Almond Cobbler

Peachy Plum Ripple

DAIRY-FREE SMOOTHIES

Banana Spinach Blast

Nutty Pumpkin Latte

Cranberry Coco Swoosh

Creamy Mango Butter

Raspberry Beet Cluster

Fruity Kale Cabana

Mixed Fruit Critters

Creamy Orange Nirvana

Minty Kiwi Gelato

Zesty Peach Paradise

HEALTHY KIDS SMOOTHIES

Peachy Pistachio

Treat Chocolaty Banana

Swirl Strawberry Banana

Twist Spinach Banana

Milano Peachy Butter

Berry Vanilla Almond

Truffle Pineapple Cherry

Craze Mixed Fruit

Ripple Vanilla Grape

Jiggles Apple Pecan Pie

LET'S FINISH STRONG!

LET'S HIT THE BODY RESET BUTTON!

I can't tell you that smoothies were my first love—because they weren't. Pulling out a smoothie maker and stocking up on all kinds of culmination and veggies simply wasn't my thing. Instead, I had a sweet tooth. So, whether or not I turned into having espresso or donuts, I continually wanted some extra sugar. I craved sugar! From my car to my handbags, sugary snacks can be without difficulty found everywhere for my very own convenience. I was like a sugar smuggler but that might exchange sooner than I realized.

Not surprisingly, my sugar addiction led to extreme weight gain, migraine headaches and low electricity levels. It wasn't encouraging to mention the least. My energy levels have been actually down to zero. I felt like I was jogging on empty. On a typical day, I could drag myself out of bed, drag myself to paintings, drag myself around the office then drag myself lower back home. Life has become a literal drag for me. Furthermore, irrespective of how a great deal I slept, I continually awakened feeling worn-out and sleepy.

Admittedly, I got uninterested in feeling worn-out. I wasn't satisfied with how I felt or how I looked. Quite frankly, I was in a 'candy' mess. As I desperately searched for a manner out of my 'sugar' dilemma, a friend of mine convinced me to sign up for her on a 10-day smoothie venture. At first, I wasn't enthusiastic about it. I become skeptical approximately being able to stick with the assignment and I changed into also involved about being sugar deprived for 10 days. Anyhow, I still decided to provide it a try. I turned into desperate for exchange! Besides, I thought, if I could alternate my life in just 10 days, then it's well worth a try.

The first 3 days of the undertaking had been most difficult. I felt as even though I couldn't make it thru without succumbing to my normal sugar cravings. I had to agonizingly refuse sugary treats at paintings and anywhere else. I felt so tortured. This turned into one of the hardest things that I ever needed to do in a protracted time. Despite all of the odds, however, I survived without cheating. Surprisingly, via day five, I had lost five pounds! Amazing isn't it? By this time, I felt surely encouraged. At the stop of 10 days, I had lost a whopping 11 pounds, my headaches had disappeared and my electricity turned into significantly improved. Interestingly, I'm now years free from my sugar addiction and loving it. Drinking these smoothies has pleasantly come to be a daily part of my life. I am now definitely convinced that ingesting smoothies is one of the easiest approaches to lose weight, increase vitality and restore fitness. If I did this, so can you!

Essentially, if you want to supercharge your fitness via making delectably healthy smoothies, then this smoothie recipe book is your solution. Whether you're a first-timer at smoothie making, an avid smoothie maker or you're just seeking out clean new methods to use your smoothie maker, you'll find exactly what you need. With a completely unique mix of various liquid bases, fruits, vegetables, nuts, seeds and spices, this e-book include a wholesome collection of nutritious and delicious recipes. You are assured that you'll be ingesting a wholesome smoothie in every glass!

FREQUENTLY ASKED QUESTIONS & ANSWERS

Confidence goes a long way with regards to making smoothies. Knowing what you are doing can make things much easier. So right here are some often asked questions & solutions approximately learning smoothie making and improving your fitness. These are the answers to the pinnacle questions that I've been requested approximately smoothies.

Why Drink Smoothies?

For me, my habit of ingesting wholesome smoothies has restored my health and kept me energized for my rapid-paced lifestyle. But there may be much more to smoothie consuming than that. By blending the proper combination of fresh culmination and vegetables, the delivered nourishment for your body is a huge benefit. Healthy smoothies are best for body cleansing, rejuvenation and restoration. Desiring to be wholesome, retaining an ideal frame weight and feeling energized are very good motives why each person would want to begin a wholesome smoothie ingesting habit. Moreover, those naturally tasty smoothies will improve your ordinary eating regimen with quick-absorbing and nutrient dense nourishment. They are additionally wealthy in phytochemicals, live enzymes, vitamins, antioxidants and numerous minerals.

Should I Drink My Glass of Smoothie Slowly?

Drinking smoothies rapid or slow doesn't really matter. Instead, I are becoming into the dependency of chewing my smoothies and I would inspire you to do the same.

Fruits and veggies are rich in fiber and may additionally once in a while have moderate bloating effects. Consequently, in order to avoid or decrease bloating and additionally aid in digestion, chewing your smoothies is usually recommended.

Which Smoothie Should I Make First?

Whatever smoothie recipe you pick from this e book is totally up to you. Based on my experience, first-timers commonly start with the fruity smoothies and then flow onto those with both end result and veggies. Green smoothies are usually a final hotel for first-timers. However, I normally recommend which you begin your smoothie regime with a inexperienced smoothie. Green smoothies are high-quality for cleansing and detoxification of the body. It makes higher sense to cleanse then nourish.

How Often Should I Drink A Smoothie?

Smoothies are meals that has been extracted or mixed into a drinkable form. Therefore, simply as you'll eat daily, you could also drink a glass or two of smoothies daily. I inspire everyone to have a glass of smoothie for breakfast every time possible. This will help to offer your frame with the right nutrients to start the day and boost your metabolism till you're geared up for your subsequent meal. However, depending on your fitness goals, you could also do not forget consuming your smoothies as a meal alternative, in-between food or with a meal. Drinking smoothies as a meal replacement is a not unusual technique for people who need to shed pounds. For the ones who would love to maintain their weight, smoothie

ingesting in-between meals is a incredible option. I don't clearly
encourage consuming a smoothie with a meal, nevertheless, 30-minutes
after a meal is quite fine.

How Can I Do a 10-Day Smoothie Challenge?

Giving your frame time to drain itself and recharge is continually a
terrific idea. Doing a 10-day smoothie mission let you to efficiently
achieve this. An best 10-day project need to include especially
inexperienced or water-based totally smoothies.

You should begin each day with a glass of warm water with a freshly
squeezed lemon or lime and give up each day with a cup of unsweetened
chamomile, dandelion or ginger tea. You need to consume green
smoothies all through every day without exceeding 64 ounces (8 cups/2
litres). Plan in advance of time and drink a glass of smoothie or have a
healthful snack on every occasion you sense hungry. Healthy snacks
include fruits, greens or a handful of uncooked nuts. Apart from healthful
snacks, you're endorsed to drink masses of purified water. No other meals
are allowed during the 10-day assignment. You may additionally do a 10-
day venture once each three months for keeping appropriate fitness.

How Can I Do a 3-Day Smoothie Detox Cleanse?

A 3-day detox cleanse is ideal for the ones who want to lose weight or
who just need a deeper cleanse. It works further to a one-day detox,
besides that it's far for three days in preference to one. You are
recommended to rotate the inexperienced smoothies every day, instead of
using the equal recipe over the extended 3-day detox period. Each day
have to begin with a pitcher of heat water with a freshly squeezed lemon
and end with a cup of chamomile, dandelion or ginger tea. You have to
consume green smoothies at some point of the three days without
exceeding sixty four ounces (8 cups/2 liters) according to day. Plan ahead
of time and drink a tumbler of smoothie or have a wholesome snack
every time you sense hungry. Apart from water and healthful snacks
which include fruits, greens or a handful of raw nuts, no other foods are
allowed in the course of the 3-day detox cleanse. You may additionally
do a 3-day cleanse every month for weight reduction and once every three
months for preserving top fitness.

What Should I Eat Following A Smoothie Challenge or Detox Cleanse?

Following a smoothie project or cleanse you are recommended to consume wholefoods (organic is nice) in preference to processed meals. You must also consume balanced meal which ought to include moderate amounts of lean (skinless and fat- trimmed) protein, lots of uncooked greens and occasional carbohydrates. In between food, you could snack on raw nuts, fruits, vegetables and drink plenty of water (enough to keep your urine pale/light colored). You may also additionally choose a high energy smoothie or freshly squeezed juice as opposed to a processed or sugar encumbered drink. Eat like this for so long as you can! You can also cheat on unique occasions or holidays.

How Do I Use These Smoothies to Lose Weight?

Many people (myself included) have lost weight using the ones smoothies.

Depending on how speedy you want to lose weight, the weight reduction method may additionally vary. If you want to take subjects gradual, you may use a weight loss smoothie to update a meal including breakfast, lunch or dinner. To make topics less complicated and flexible, you have to pick to replace a meal at a time most handy for you (morning, midday or evening). You can try this meal alternative daily till you start to see the results that you are searching for. If you need speedy weight loss, you must do a 10-day smoothie task or 3-day smoothie detox in line with the guidelines mentioned earlier. For weight reduction, you can pick recipes from the weight reduction smoothies and/or the inexperienced smoothie categories.

What is Unique about Your Smoothie Book?

The Smoothie Maker Recipe Book is NOT just another recipe e book of smoothie recipes. These recipes include carefully decided on substances which is probably geared toward specific fitness dreams for your first-rate advantage. All the recipes are calorie counted and comprise measurements which is probably best to each US and UK consumers. Overall, the e-book is a nice desire for those who want to make healthful smoothies without compromising an excessive amount of on taste.

How do you store your lovely smoothies?

I leave my leftover smoothies inside the fridge if I am planning on the use of it the same day. If I need to save it for the following day, I preserve it the freezer compartment and thaw it inside the refrigerator on every occasion I need it.

What are the most Smoothie Ingredients you like?

I typically tend to like recipes with a mixture of veggies leafy veggies and culmination. And I'll let you know why. I actually don't want to consume most greens. Hence, the fruit and vegetable blends are a fantastic manner for me to eat my greens without experiencing the overpowering taste. Also, I have noticed that the smoothies with a combination of culmination and vegetables make me revel in much greater energized.

What Sweeteners Should I Use In My Smoothies?

Fruits have their own sweetness, so if you may tolerate it, I would encourage you to avoid or minimize the quantity of brought sugars in your smoothies. However, in case you think your smoothie wishes that added sugar boost, you could opt for healthier sweeteners along with honey, maple syrup, agave nectar, stevia, dates and other high-sugar culmination. Always use sweeteners in moderation.

Any Smoothie Preparation Tips?

Make a shopping listing and move purchasing for specific recipe components which you do not have at home. Whenever you go shopping always pick out sparkling (natural is best) produce and purchase a little extra anyplace possible. Always acquire, put together and element out the recipe substances for the smoothie that you need to make. Remember to usually wash your produce. Follow that the recipe directions very well. If you want delivered sweetness, you have to upload, combo and flavor, rather than adding all of it at once. Clean up immediately or as soon as you may.

How Can I Make My Smoothie Morning Regime Easier?

If you are attempting to make your morning smoothie habit easier, it will virtually help in case you acquire, prepare and portion out the recipe elements for the smoothie from the night before. By doing this, all you must do within the morning is run your smoothie maker and in three minutes or less, you're done.

What Sources of Fats Do You Use in Your Smoothies?

There are many resources of healthy fats that can be used in smoothies. I support using healthy fats in smoothies because it's miles a exceptional protection net for multiplied nutrient absorption and delivered power boost. Some of the introduced fats in my smoothies include avocados, nuts, seeds and nut butters.

What Liquid Base Do You Use in Your Smoothies?

I do no longer support using processed liquids in my smoothies due to the hidden sugar component and the hazard of other harmful brought ingredients. The liquid base that you'll find in these recipes encompass: fresh and unsweetened fruit juices, purified water, natural unsweetened coconut water, dairy and non-dairy milk. Feel free to make you preferred non-dairy milk substitutions primarily based on your private flavor and preference.

How Can I Make My Smoothies Thicker or Thinner?

You could make your smoothies thicker or thinner via making a few mild changes to 3 elements. For thicker smoothies, you can upload much less liquid than required, add much less ice, use frozen culmination or in reality procedure your smoothie for a shorter time period. While for thinner smoothies, you can upload greater liquid and use clean culmination then manner simply enough until smooth.

What Can I Do If I Don't Like a Smoothie?

First off, if you don't need to use culmination and greens in your smoothies, this smoothie e-book isn't for you. Depending on the ingredients and your taste palate, some smoothies may also seem a bit sweet, no longer sweet sufficient, a bit tangy, or not creamy enough. If the smoothie seems too sweet, you may add a teaspoon of lemon or lime juice, upload extra ice, or upload a little water. If your smoothie is not sweet sufficient, you could upload healthier sweeteners which include honey, maple syrup, agave nectar, stevia, dates and different high-sugar end result. If your smoothie is just too tangy, you may use neutralizing culmination like bananas or mangos and a tablespoon of your preferred protein powder. For delivered creaminess, you can add fruits like avocados or simply truly upload a few yogurts.

What Can I Do if I Want To Make A Single Serving Smoothie?

It is authentic that it's difficult to make a scrumptious glass of smoothie and hold all of it to you. For this reason, these recipes are for two servings. Nevertheless, if you sincerely want to make a single serving smoothie, you ought to use half of every required aspect in any given recipe. For example, if the recipe calls for 1 cup milk and 1 banana, you will use ½ cup milk and ½ bananas for 1 serving. By doing this, you will still keep an excellent smoothie consistency and get similar results.

LET'S GET STARTED

With The Smoothie Maker Recipe Book you can use your smoothie maker or blender to make daily, weekly or periodic smoothies that will help you keep properly health. So, whether or not you need to lose weight or just simple need to energise your frame, there is a smoothie in this ebook just for you. I've always believed that there's no need to kick-off a new year with wholesome habits. Instead, I agree with that we all deserve a healthful start each day. So, be a part of me and let's do this. Choose a recipe, collect your elements and begin consuming a few first rate healthful smoothies. Let's now hit the body reset button with those smoothies!

HEALTHY BRAIN SMOOTHIES

Blueberry Avocado Smash

This exquisite blueberry and avocado smoothie is full of scrumptious and healthy substances which can be all excellent for reinforcing brain electricity and vitality.

MAKES: 2 servings

PREPARATION TIME: 10 minutes

Calories consistent with serving: 318

1 cup/240ml unsweetened Almond Milk 2 cups/290g Fresh Blueberries

1 small Avocado, peeled, pitted and chopped 1 tablespoon Chia Seeds

4 Ice Cubes

Directions

Add the almond milk to a smoothie maker or blender. Add the last substances and pulse until smooth.

Start drinking the smoothie into 2 glasses & serve immediately.

Flax Strawberry Strip

This smoothie is a scrumptious mixture of appetizing ingredients. The strawberries in this recipe properly praise the fresh apple juice, yogurt and flaxseed oil.

MAKES: 2 servings

PREPARATION TIME: 10 minutes

Calories according to serving: 316

1¼ cups/300ml Fresh Apple juice

¼ cup/60ml Plain Yogurt

2 tablespoons Flaxseed Oil

2 cups/290g Strawberries, frozen

1 small Banana, peeled, sliced and frozen

4 Ice Cubes

Directions

Add the apple juice to a smoothie maker or blender. Add the last ingredients and pulse till smooth.

Start drinking the smoothie into 2 glasses & serve immediately.

Creamy Kiwi Cooler

This recipe is a healthy green smoothie which is good for the whole family. It is a high-quality tasting manner to get plenty of useful vitamins and flavors into your diet.

MAKES: 2 servings

PREPARATION TIME: 10 minutes

Calories in keeping with serving: 399

1 cup/240ml Fresh Apple juice 1 cup/240ml Frozen Kefir

1 medium Cucumber, peeled and chopped 2 cups/60g Fresh Baby Spinach

1 big Kiwi, peeled and chopped

1 small Avocado, peeled, pitted and chopped Stevia or preferred sweetener, to taste (optional)

1 tablespoon Flaxseeds

4 Ice Cubes (optional)

Directions

Add the apple juice and kefir to a smoothie maker or blender. Add the final substances and pulse till smooth.

Start drinking the smoothie into 2 glasses & serve immediately.

Creamy Acai Mango

This smoothie is a wonderful blend of mango and avocado which makes an incredibly tasty and creamy drink. You'll feel the difference!

MAKES: 2 servings

REPARATION TIME: 10 minutes

Calories consistent with serving: 425

2 cups/480ml Soy Milk

2 cups/60g Fresh Spinach, chopped

1 small Avocado, peeled, pitted and chopped 1 medium Mango, peeled, pitted and chopped

Stevia or preferred sweetener, to taste (optional)

½ tablespoon Acai Powder

4 Ice Cubes

Directions

Add the soy milk to a smoothie maker or blender. Add the final elements and pulse till smooth.

Start drinking the smoothie into 2 glasses & serve immediately.

Banana Mixed Berry

This recipe uses a combination of notable tasting pomegranate juice and fresh berries. This smoothie not simplest boosts your mind health but it's also unbeatable in flavor and nutrition.

MAKES: 2 servings

PREPARATION TIME: 10 minutes

Calories consistent with serving: 275

1¼ cups/300ml Fresh Pomegranate juice 1 cup/145g Fresh Raspberries

2 cups/290g Fresh Blueberries

1 small Banana, peeled, sliced and frozen 2 tablespoons Chia Seeds

4 Ice Cubes

Directions

Add the pomegranate juice to a smoothie maker or blender. Add the ultimate elements and pulse till smooth.

Start consuming the smoothie into 2 glasses & serve immediately.

Apple Blackberry Spin

This fruity smoothie has a wonderful rich texture furnished via the pumpkin seeds and almonds. This smoothie is quite scrumptious and a exceptional raise on your brain!

MAKES: 2 servings

PREPARATION TIME: 10 minutes

Calories in line with serving: 380

1½ cups/360ml Fresh Apple juice 2 Apples, peeled, cored and chopped

½ cup/73g Blackberries, frozen 1 large Banana, peeled and sliced

three tablespoons Pumpkin Seeds

3 tablespoons Almonds, chopped

4 Ice Cubes

Directions

Add the apple juice to a smoothie maker or blender. Add the closing substances and pulse till smooth.

Start ingesting the smoothie into 2 glasses & serve immediately.

Spiced Banana Flex

This fresh kale and banana smoothie is loaded with wholesome nutrients. The addition of the spices and almond butter provides a awesome texture to this smoothie.

MAKES: 2 servings

PREPARATION TIME: 10 minutes

Calories in step with serving: 784

2 cups/480ml Almond Milk

four cups/172g Fresh Kale, trimmed and chopped 1 massive Banana, peeled, sliced and frozen

2 tablespoons Almond Butter

¼ teaspoon Ground Ginger

¼ teaspoon Ground Cinnamon

¼ teaspoon Ground Nutmeg

4 Ice Cubes

Directions

Add the almond milk to a smoothie maker or blender. Add the last ingredients and pulse until smooth.

Start drinking the smoothie into 2 glasses & serve immediately.

Peacho Cabana

This smoothie, a combination of peach and banana with sparkling apple juice and yogurt, grants a definitely flavorful smoothie in minutes.

MAKES: 2 servings

PREPARATION TIME: 10 minutes

Calories according to serving: 228

1 cup/240ml Fresh Apple juice

¼ cup/60ml Plain Yogurt

2 Peaches, peeled, pitted and chopped 1 massive Banana, peeled and sliced

2 teaspoons Flaxseed Oil

1-2 drops Liquid Stevia (optional) 1 teaspoon Vanilla Extract

4 Ice Cubes

Directions

Add the apple juice and yogurt to a smoothie maker or blender. Add the remaining substances and pulse till smooth.

Start drinking the smoothie into 2 glasses & serve immediately.

Blueberry Kale Goodness

This deliciously sweet smoothie is packed with nutritional ingredients of kale, blueberries, banana and almonds. This is a incredible brain drink!

MAKES: 2 servings

PREPARATION TIME: 10 minutes

Calories consistent with serving: 771

2 cups/480ml Almond Milk

2 cups/290g Blueberries, frozen

1 small Banana, peeled, sliced and frozen 2 cups/86g Fresh Baby Kale

¼ cup/24g Almonds, chopped

2-3 drops Liquid Stevia or preferred sweetener (optional)

4 Ice Cubes

Directions

Add the almond milk to a smoothie maker or blender. Add the remaining elements and pulse till smooth.

Start drinking the smoothie into 2 glasses & serve immediately.

Strawberry Kiwi Jiggle

This recipe makes a delicious and wholesome fruit drink for smoothie lovers. The use of chia seeds gives this smoothie extra power and texture.

MAKES: 2 servings

PREPARATION TIME: 10 minutes

Calories according to serving: 570

1½ cups/360ml Almond Milk

1 large Kiwi, peeled and chopped 2 cups/290g Strawberries, frozen

1 medium Banana, peeled and sliced 2 tablespoons Chia Seeds

4 Ice Cubes

Directions

Add the almond milk to a smoothie maker or blender. Add the closing elements and pulse till smooth.

Start drinking the smoothie into 2 glasses & serve immediately.

Mixed Chia Berry

This vanilla flavored smoothie, being made with fresh berries, is splendidly fruity. You will revel in this chia enhanced smoothie for breakfast time and again!

MAKES: 2 servings

PREPARATION TIME: five minutes

Calories according to serving: 160

1 cup/240ml Milk

1 cup/145g Fresh Blueberries

1 cup/145g Fresh Strawberries, hulled and sliced 2 tablespoons Chia Seeds

1 teaspoon Vanilla

4 Ice Cubes

Directions

In a smoothie maker or blender, add all of the substances and pulse until smooth.

Start ingesting the smoothie into 2 glasses & serve immediately.

Raspberry Red Fusion

This is a vibrantly coloured smoothie with a highly-priced texture. This crimson smoothie is chock complete with the antioxidant advantages of crimson beets and raspberries.

MAKES: 2 servings

PREPARATION TIME: 10 minutes

Calories in step with serving: 157

1 cup/240ml Fresh Cranberry juice, chilled

½ cup/120ml Plain Yogurt

1 massive Beet, trimmed, peeled and chopped

½ cup/73g Raspberries, frozen

Directions

In a smoothie maker or blender, add all of the components and pulse until smooth.

If you want to keep away from the excess fiber in this smoothie, you could use a fine sieve to pressure the smoothie.

Start ingesting the smoothie into 2 glasses & serve immediately.

Pomegranate Merry Berry

This delicious breakfast smoothie is filled with clean berries and pomegranate juice. This tasty and fulfilling smoothie might also satisfy all who drink it!

MAKES: 2 servings

PREPARATION TIME: 10 minutes

Calories in step with serving: 153

1 cup/240ml unsweetened Fresh Pomegranate Juice

½ cup/120ml Filtered Water 1 cup/145g Fresh Raspberries 1 cup/145g Fresh Blackberries

1 tablespoon Chia Seeds

Directions

In a smoothie maker or blender, upload the pomegranate juice and water. Add the final substances and pulse till smooth.

Start consuming the smoothie into 2 glasses & serve immediately.

Spiced Mango Vanilla

This recipe makes a tasty and healthful smoothie which is right for breakfast. This mango smoothie can be a morning superb treat for mango lovers.

MAKES: 2 servings

PREPARATION TIME: 10 minutes

Calories according to serving: 231

1¼ cups/300ml Milk

2 Mangoes, peeled, pitted and chopped 1 teaspoon Cinnamon Extract

1 teaspoon Vanilla Extract

4 Ice Cubes

Directions

In a smoothie maker or blender, add all the ingredients and pulse until smooth.

Start drinking the smoothie into 2 glasses & serve immediately.

Raspy Strawberry Tang

This recipe makes a wonderfully delicious breakfast drink. The strawberries and raspberries used in this recipe are blended with the sparkling orange juice to create a splendidly delicious treat.

MAKES: 2 servings

PREPARATION TIME: 10 minutes

Calories in line with serving: 182

1 cup/240ml Fresh Orange juice 1 cup/240ml Plain Yogurt

1 cup/145g Fresh Strawberries, hulled and sliced

½ cup/73g Fresh Raspberries

four Ice Cubes

Directions

In a smoothie maker or blender, upload all the ingredients and pulse till smooth.

Start drinking the smoothie into 2 glasses & serve immediately.

Tropical Papanilla

This scrumptious fruit smoothie is full of the tropical flavors of papaya. It may also be served with a serving of your favorite chopped fruits.

MAKES: 2 servings

PREPARATION TIME: 10 minutes

Calories according to serving: 116

1¼ cups/300ml Milk

½ medium Papaya, peeled, seeded and chopped

1 tablespoon Agave Nectar, or desired sweetener (optional)

¼ teaspoon Vanilla Extract

4 Ice Cubes

Directions

In a smoothie maker or blender, add all the components and pulse till smooth.

Start consuming the smoothie into 2 glasses & serve immediately.

Fruity Almond Sip

Start your day with a candy and creamy smoothie. The use of almond butter adds a creamy touch to this fruity smoothie.

MAKES: 2 servings

PREPARATION TIME: 10 minutes

Calories in keeping with serving: 439

1½ cups/360ml Milk

1½ cups/218g Raspberries, frozen 1 medium Banana, peeled and sliced

2 tablespoons Almond Butter

Directions

In a smoothie maker or blender, upload all the ingredients and pulse until smooth.

Start drinking the smoothie into 2 glasses & serve immediately.

Banana Spiced Oatmeal

This is a scrumptious smoothie with a touch of cinnamon. This cereal-like banana smoothie is made with milk and vanilla extract and spiked with cinnamon.

MAKES: 2 servings

PREPARATION TIME: 10 minutes

Calories in keeping with serving: 186

1½ cups/360ml Milk

1 big Banana, peeled, sliced and frozen

1 teaspoon Vanilla Extract

¼ teaspoon Ground Nutmeg 3 tablespoons Oatmeal

4 Ice Cubes

Directions

In a smoothie maker or blender, upload all the components and pulse till smooth.

Start consuming the smoothie into 2 glasses & serve immediately.

Vanilla Berry Surprise

This is a mouthwatering smoothie this is packed with added omega-3 vitamins from the flax seeds. This fruity smoothie will come up with a little more improve for the entire day.

MAKES: 2 servings

PREPARATION TIME: 10 minutes

Calories in step with serving: 242

1 cup/240ml Fresh Juice (use your preferred)

½ cup/120ml Vanilla Yogurt

2 cups/290g Strawberries, hulled, sliced and frozen 1 medium Banana, peeled and sliced

3 tablespoons Flax Seeds

Directions

In a smoothie maker or blender, upload all of the ingredients and pulse until smooth.

Start ingesting the smoothie into 2 glasses & serve immediately.

Slimming Citrus Swirl

This is a high-quality and refreshing smoothie for orange lovers. This drink is a fun way to start out your morning in a delicious way!

MAKES: 2 servings

PREPARATION TIME: 10 minutes

Calories according to serving: 123

1 cup/240ml Low-Fat Milk

1 medium Orange, peeled, seeded and sectioned 1 medium Grapefruit, peeled, seeded and sectioned

2 tablespoons Stevia or preferred sweetener (optional)

4 Ice Cubes

Directions

In a smoothie maker or blender, upload all the ingredients and pulse until smooth.

Start ingesting the smoothie into 2 glasses & serve immediately.

Rich Tropicana Pine

This recipe makes a tropical fruit smoothie with only some ingredients. This easy breakfast smoothie may be a brilliant hit for the complete family.

MAKES: 2 servings

PREPARATION TIME: 10 minutes

Calories according to serving: 242

1 cup/240ml Milk

1 cup/240ml Plain Yogurt

1 cup/165g Fresh Pineapple Chunks 1 medium Banana, peeled and sliced

4 Ice Cubes

Directions

In a smoothie maker or blender, upload all the ingredients and pulse until smooth.

Start ingesting the smoothie into 2 glasses & serve immediately.

Watermelon Fruit Fiddle

This is a light and refreshing smoothie with the taste of summer! You may additionally upload a cup of your favourite juice in this combo to make it even more interesting.

MAKES: 2 servings

PREPARATION TIME: 10 minutes

Calories consistent with serving: 98

1 cup/152g Watermelon, peeled, seeded and cubed 1 cup/145g Mixed Berries, frozen

1 Gala Apple, seeded and chopped

4 Ice Cubes

Directions

In a smoothie maker or blender, add all the elements and pulse until smooth.

Start consuming the smoothie into 2 glasses & serve immediately.

Citrus Carrot Flakes

This is a wholesome smoothie that is full of vitamins and beta carotene. The mixture of fresh orange juice with carrots presents a super tasting smoothie.

MAKES: 2 servings

PREPARATION TIME: 10 minutes

Calories in line with serving: 129

1½ cups/360ml Fresh Orange juice

½ cup/120ml Filtered Water

2 cups/220g Carrots, peeled and chopped

½ teaspoon Orange Peel, freshly grated

4 Ice Cubes

Directions

Add the orange juice and water to a smoothie maker or blender.

Add the last substances and pulse till smooth.

Start drinking the smoothie into 2 glasses & serve immediately.

Beet Breeze Trim

This is a weight reduction pleasant smoothie with tomato and beets. This drink is rich in fiber and really nutritious.

MAKES: 2 servings

PREPARATION TIME: 10 minutes

Calories in line with serving: 125

1½ cups/360ml Organic Coconut Water 1 Beet, peeled and chopped

1 massive Tomato, chopped

1 Banana, peeled, sliced and frozen Sweetener, to taste (optional)

4 Ice Cubes

Directions

Add the coconut water to a smoothie maker or blender. Add the closing ingredients and pulse till smooth.

Start drinking the smoothie into 2 glasses & serve immediately.

Cherry Tomato Surprise

This smoothie is full of deliciously healthy and fantastically purple colored ingredients. You can be amazed at how fine this smoothie tastes and it'll quickly emerge as a fave drink.

MAKES: 2 servings

PREPARATION TIME: 10 minutes

Calories consistent with serving: 245

2 cups/480ml Coconut Water 1 large Tomato, chopped

1 cup/180g Fresh Cherries, pitted 1½ cups/138g Seedless Red Grapes

4 Ice Cubes

Directions

Add the coconut water to a smoothie maker or blender. Add the last ingredients and pulse till smooth.

Start drinking the smoothie into 2 glasses & serve immediately.

Spinach Apple Burner

This smoothie is a brief and clean recipe for the entire family. It is a first-rate manner to get your every-day improves of strength from extraordinary foods.

MAKES: 2 servings

PREPARATION TIME: 10 minutes

Calories per serving: 129

1½ cups/360ml Filtered Water

1 big Apple, peeled, cored and chopped 2 cups/290g Raspberries

2 cups/60g Fresh Spinach, chopped

4 Ice Cubes

Directions

Add the water to a smoothie maker or blender. Add the final elements and pulse until smooth.

Start drinking the smoothie into 2 glasses & serve immediately.

Fruity Kale Splash

This smoothie, combining the flavor and nutrients of sparkling culmination and veggies in a single drink, is a exquisite mixture of fruits and vegetables.

MAKES: 2 servings

PREPARATION TIME: 10 minutes

Calories per serving: 185

1½ cups/360ml Filtered Water

1 Pear, peeled, cored and chopped

1 massive Apple, peeled, cored and chopped 1 Banana, peeled, sliced and frozen

1 Celery Stalk, chopped

2 cups/86g Fresh Kale, trimmed

4 Ice Cubes

Directions

Add the water to a smoothie maker or blender. Add the closing elements and pulse until smooth.

Start drinking the smoothie into 2 glasses & serve immediately.

Creamy Apple & Blueberry

This is a creamy, textured smoothie with none dairy products. The apples, blueberries and avocado mixture greatly together and deliver a exquisite taste on this smoothie.

MAKES: 2 servings

PREPARATION TIME: 10 minutes

Calories per serving: 251

1½ cups/360ml Filtered Water 2 cups/290g Blueberries, frozen

1 big Apple, peeled, cored and chopped

½ Avocado, peeled, pitted and chopped 2 cups/60g Fresh Baby Spinach

4 Ice Cubes

Directions

Add the water to a smoothie maker or blender. Add the ultimate components and pulse till smooth.

Start drinking the smoothie into 2 glasses & serve immediately.

Mixed Apple Energy

This recipe makes a refreshingly healthy smoothie. This drink will quickly turn out to be a corporation favourite for all weight watchers!

MAKES: 2 servings

PREPARATION TIME: 10 minutes

Calories per serving: 181

1½ cups/360ml Filtered Water

3 huge Apples, peeled, cored and chopped 3 cups/90g Mixed Fresh Greens

1 Celery Stalk, chopped

4 Ice Cubes

Directions

Add the water to a smoothie maker or blender. Add the ultimate components and pulse till smooth.

Start drinking the smoothie into 2 glasses & serve immediately.

Strawberry Pear Sherbet

This is a delicious smoothie with an adorable creamy touch. The strawberries in this drink offer a scrumptious complementary flavor to the pear and avocado.

MAKES: 2 servings

PREPARATION TIME: 10 minutes

Calories per serving: 334

½ cup/120ml Filtered Water

1 cup/240ml Fat-Free Plain Yogurt 1½ cups/218g Strawberries

2 Pears, peeled, cored and chopped

½ small Avocado, peeled, pitted and chopped

4 Ice Cubes

Directions

Add the water to a smoothie maker or blender. Add the closing elements and pulse until smooth.

Start consuming the smoothie into 2 glasses & serve immediately.

Blueberry Pineapple Custard

This recipe makes a well flavored and refreshing smoothie. The use of fresh child spinach on this drink presents an extra healthy punch with the pineapple and blueberries.

MAKES: 2 servings

PREPARATION TIME: 10 minutes

Calories in line with serving: 188

1½ cups/360ml Filtered Water

½ cup/120ml Fat-Free Plain Yogurt 2 cups/330g Pineapple Chunks, frozen

1½ cups/218g Blueberries, frozen 2 cups/60g Fresh Baby Spinach

4 Ice Cubes

Directions

Add the water to a smoothie maker or blender. Add the closing components and pulse till smooth.

Start drinking the smoothie into 2 glasses & serve immediately.

Papaya & Kale Sunset

This is a first-rate tropical deal with! The sparkling Kale affords extra antioxidant vitamins on this delicious tropical smoothie.

MAKES: 2 servings

PREPARATION TIME: 10 minutes

Calories per serving: 215

2 cups/480ml Chilled Coconut Water

½ cup/120ml Fat-Free Yogurt

2 cups/330g Pineapple Chunks, frozen 1 cup/140g Papaya, peeled and chopped

2 cups/86g Fresh Kale, trimmed and chopped

4 Ice Cubes

Directions

Add the coconut water to a smoothie maker or blender. Add the last elements and pulse till smooth.

Start drinking the smoothie into 2 glasses & serve immediately.

Cool Green Garden

This is a scrumptious and fresh aggregate of garden clean elements. The addition of clean mint leaves adds a unique freshness to this smoothie.

MAKES: 2 servings

PREPARATION TIME: 10 minutes

Calories in line with serving: 92

1½ cups/360ml Filtered Water

½ cup/120ml Fat-Free Yogurt

1 Green Apple, peeled, cored and chopped 1 cup/104g Cucumber, peeled and chopped 2 tablespoons Fresh Mint Leaves

4 Ice Cubes

Directions

Add the water and to a smoothie maker or blender. Add the ultimate components and pulse till smooth.

Start eating the smoothie into 2 glasses & serve immediately.

Mixed Fruit Spinach

This is a delicious and best deal with for a hot summer season day. This nutritious smoothie might be enjoyed by way of all who flavor it.

MAKES: 2 servings

PREPARATION TIME: 10 minutes

Calories according to serving: 174

1½ cups/360ml Chilled Coconut Water

2 cups/304g Watermelon, seeded and chopped 1 cup/165g Pineapple chunks, frozen

1 massive Green Apple, peeled, cored and chopped 1 cup/30g Fresh Spinach

Directions

Add the coconut water to a smoothie maker or blender. Add the ultimate substances and pulse until smooth.

Start eating the smoothie into 2 glasses & serve immediately.

Cool Green Garden

This is a scrumptious and fresh aggregate of garden clean elements. The addition of clean mint leaves adds a unique freshness to this smoothie.

MAKES: 2 servings

PREPARATION TIME: 10 minutes

Calories in line with serving: 92

1½ cups/360ml Filtered Water

½ cup/120ml Fat-Free Yogurt

1 Green Apple, peeled, cored and chopped 1 cup/104g Cucumber, peeled and chopped 2 tablespoons Fresh Mint Leaves

4 Ice Cubes

Directions

Add the water and to a smoothie maker or blender. Add the ultimate components and pulse till smooth.

Start eating the smoothie into 2 glasses & serve immediately.

Mixed Fruit Spinach

This is a delicious and best deal with for a hot summer season day. This nutritious smoothie might be enjoyed by way of all who flavor it.

MAKES: 2 servings

PREPARATION TIME: 10 minutes

Calories according to serving: 174

1½ cups/360ml Chilled Coconut Water

2 cups/304g Watermelon, seeded and chopped 1 cup/165g Pineapple chunks, frozen

1 massive Green Apple, peeled, cored and chopped 1 cup/30g Fresh Spinach

Directions

Add the coconut water to a smoothie maker or blender. Add the ultimate substances and pulse until smooth.

Start drinking the smoothie into 2 glasses & serve immediately.

GREEN SMOOTHIES

Zesty Avocado Mango

This recipe makes a refreshing creamy deal with for summer. The use of avocado gives this smoothie a creamy texture without using any additional dairy products.

MAKES: 2 servings

PREPARATION TIME: 10 minutes

Calories in line with serving: 240

1½ cups/360ml Filtered Water

1 medium Avocado, peeled, pitted and chopped 1 cup Ripe Mango, cubed

1 teaspoon Lime Zest, freshly grated

4 Ice Cubes

Directions

Add the water to a smoothie maker or blender. Add the final components and pulse till smooth.

Start drinking the smoothie into 2 glasses & serve immediately.

Spinach Berry Refresh

This is a refreshingly scrumptious smoothie this is splendidly nutritious. This recipe properly combines tasty berries with healthful spinach.

MAKES: 2 servings

PREPARATION TIME: 10 minutes

Calories in line with serving: 69

1½ cups/360ml Filtered Water 2 cups/60g Fresh Baby Spinach 1 cup/145g Fresh Berries

1 tablespoon Hemp Seeds

½ teaspoon Ground Cinnamon

four Ice Cubes

Directions

Add the water to a smoothie maker or blender. Add the remaining ingredients, besides for the cinnamon, and pulse till smooth.

Start drinking the smoothie into 2 glasses & serve immediately.

Mixed Greens Pineapple

This very low calorie smoothie has a pleasing combination of green greens and pineapple. This drink will not only fulfill any hunger, it will additionally make you experience energized and happy!

MAKES: 2 servings

PREPARATION TIME: 10 minutes

Calories in keeping with serving: 77

1½ cups/360ml Filtered Water

1 tablespoon Fresh Lemon juice

½ medium Cucumber, peeled and chopped three Fresh Kale Leaves, trimmed and chopped

½ cup/83g Pineapple Chunks

1 tablespoon Maple Syrup or desired sweetener (optional)

4 Ice Cubes

Directions

Add the water and lemon juice right into a smoothie maker or blender. Add the closing ingredients and pulse till smooth.

Start drinking the smoothie into 2 glasses & serve immediately.

Kale Banana Mist

This smoothie, being a blend of inexperienced leafy veggies, is a tasty manner to squeeze an additional serving of veggies into your each day diet.

MAKES: 2 servings

PREPARATION TIME: 10 minutes

Calories consistent with serving: 136

1½ cups/360ml Coconut Water 1 cup/30g Fresh Spinach, chopped

1 cup/67g Fresh Kale, trimmed and chopped 2 small Bananas, peeled and sliced

4 Ice Cubes

Directions

Add the coconut water to a smoothie maker or blender. Add the ultimate ingredients and pulse until smooth.

Start drinking the smoothie into 2 glasses & serve immediately.

Kiwi Pear Crush

This smoothie blends the delicious flavors of pear and kiwi fruit with vegetables to make a sweet and delightfully fruity smoothie for the entire family.

MAKES: 2 servings

PREPARATION TIME: 10 minutes

Calories per serving: 200

1½ cups/360ml Filtered Water

1 medium Pear, peeled, cored and chopped 4 Kiwis, peeled and chopped

1 big Banana, peeled and sliced 1 cup/45g Collard Greens

4 Ice Cubes

Directions

Add the water to a smoothie maker or blender. Add the last substances and pulse till smooth.

Start drinking the smoothie into 2 glasses & serve immediately.

Mint Mango Summer

This recipe makes a satisfying and delicious smoothie loaded with wholesome vitamins. In this smoothie the superb flavors of kiwi, mango, kale, celery and mint are superbly combined.

MAKES: 2 servings

PREPARATION TIME: 10 minutes

Calories consistent with serving: 172

1½ cups/360ml Filtered Water

1 Mango, peeled, pitted and chopped 2 Kiwis, peeled and chopped

3 cups/201g Fresh Baby Kale, trimmed 1 small Celery Stalk, chopped

2 tablespoons Fresh Mint Leaves

4 Ice Cubes

Directions

Add the water to a smoothie maker or blender. Add the remaining elements and pulse till smooth.

Start drinking the smoothie into 2 glasses & serve immediately.

Celery Wonder Punch

This is a simple and excellent tasting manner to introduce wholesome vitamins into your diet. This smoothie is a incredible mixture of fruits and greens.

MAKES: 2 servings

PREPARATION TIME: 10 minutes

Calories consistent with serving: 146

1½ cups/360ml Filtered Water

1 Pear, peeled, cored and chopped

1 Green Apple, peeled, cored and chopped 1 medium Banana, peeled and sliced

1 cup/30g Fresh Spinach, chopped 2 Celery Stalks, chopped

4 Ice Cubes (optional)

Directions

Add the water into a smoothie maker or blender. Add the last ingredients and pulse until smooth.

Start drinking the smoothie into 2 glasses & serve immediately.

Pineapple Spinach Splash

This is a totally low calorie recipe which makes a wonderfully delicious, refreshing and healthy smoothie. The aggregate of kiwi and pineapple provides a natural sweetness to this smoothie.

MAKES: 2 servings

PREPARATION TIME: 10 minutes

Calories in keeping with serving: 78

1½ cups/360ml Filtered Water

2 cups/60g Fresh Spinach, chopped 1 Kiwi, peeled and chopped

1 cup/165g Pineapple Chunks, frozen

1 teaspoon Hemp Seeds

Directions

Add the water into a smoothie maker or blender. Add the closing substances and pulse until smooth.

Start drinking the smoothie into 2 glasses & serve immediately.

Mixed Apple Jubilee

This recipe makes a candy smoothie that is filled with the flavors of apple, banana and baby greens. This smoothie is assured to come to be one among your favorites.

MAKES: 2 servings

PREPARATION TIME: 10 minutes

Calories in keeping with serving: 117

1½ cups/360ml Filtered Water

1 Green Apple, peeled, cored and chopped 1 big Banana, peeled, sliced and frozen 1 cup/45g Mixed Fresh Baby Greens

1 Medjool Date, pitted and chopped (optional)

4 Ice Cubes

Directions

Add the water to a smoothie maker or blender. Add the ultimate substances and pulse until smooth.

Start drinking the smoothie into 2 glasses & serve immediately.

Green Ginger Candy

This is a splendidly delicious way to revel in a healthful drink! The sparkling ginger has anti-inflammatory benefits and adds a further healthy kick to the combination of fruit and vegetables.

MAKES: 2 servings

PREPARATION TIME: 10 minutes

Calories per serving: 187

1½ cups/360ml Coconut Water

1 Green Apple, peeled, cored and chopped 1½ cups/51g Fresh Kale, chopped

1 medium Cucumber, peeled and chopped

¼ teaspoon Fresh Ginger, chopped

2 tablespoons Fresh Parsley Leaves

2 tablespoons Honey or favored sweetener (optional)

4 Ice Cubes

Directions

Add the coconut water to a smoothie maker or blender. Add the ultimate ingredients and pulse until smooth.

Start drinking the smoothie into 2 glasses & serve immediately.

Apple Vanilla Crunch

This wealthy and creamy smoothie is filled with apples, walnuts and protein powder. This recipe makes a delicious and fiber-rich smoothie.

MAKES: 2 servings

PREPARATION TIME: 10 minutes

Calories in keeping with serving: 375

2 cups/480ml Milk

2 medium Apples, peeled, cored and chopped

2 tablespoons Ground Flaxseed

2 tablespoons Walnuts, chopped

1 scoop Unsweetened Protein Powder

1 teaspoon Honey or favored sweetener (optional)

1 teaspoon Vanilla Extract

½ teaspoon Ground Cinnamon

4 Ice Cubes

Directions

Add the milk to a smoothie maker or blender. Add the ultimate ingredients and pulse until smooth.

Start drinking the smoothie into 2 glasses & serve immediately.

Nutty Spiced Banana

This recipe wonderfully blends banana with other delicious and wholesome meals components to make a power-packed drink. The use of cinnamon and nutmeg adds a nice warm contact to this smoothie.

MAKES: 2 servings

PREPARATION TIME: 10 minutes

Calories in step with serving: 250

¾ cup/180ml Milk

½ cup/120ml Plain Yogurt

1 huge Banana, peeled and sliced 2 tablespoons Almonds, chopped

1 scoop Unsweetened Protein Powder

1 teaspoon Maple Syrup or preferred sweetener (optional)

¼ teaspoon Ground Nutmeg

4 Ice Cubes

Directions

Add the milk to a smoothie maker or blender. Add the remaining substances and pulse until smooth.

Start drinking the smoothie into 2 glasses & serve immediately.

Cherry Blueberry Jiggle

This smoothie is a joyful combination of grapes and blueberries. The addition of a scoop of protein powder will help you meet your day by day protein requirement and growth your metabolism.

MAKES: 2 servings

PREPARATION TIME: 10 minutes

Calories per serving: 316

1½ cups/360ml Unsweetened Cherry juice 2 cups/290g Blueberries, frozen

1 cup/92g Seedless Red Grapes

1 scoop unsweetened Vanilla flavored Protein Powder 2 teaspoons Chia Seeds

4 Ice Cubes

Directions

In a smoothie maker or blender, add all the substances and pulse till smooth.

Start drinking the smoothie into 2 glasses & serve immediately.

Citrus Banana Zest

This smoothie is a pleasing combo of banana and fresh orange juice. You will locate this clean smoothie to be tremendous tasting and fulfilling.

MAKES: 2 servings

PREPARATION TIME: 10 minutes

Calories consistent with serving: 249

1½ cups/360ml Milk

½ cup/a hundred and twenty ml Fresh Orange Juice 1 frozen Banana, peeled and sliced

1 scoop Unsweetened Protein Powder

1 teaspoon Orange Zest, freshly grated

2 teaspoons Honey or preferred sweetener (optional)

4 Ice Cubes

Directions

Add the milk and orange juice to a smoothie maker or blender. Add the last components and pulse until smooth.

Start drinking the smoothie into 2 glasses & serve immediately.

Gingery Papaya Power

This smoothie is a awesome mixture of yogurt, papaya, ginger and maple syrup. This drink is not best surprisingly scrumptious; it's also full of healthy protein substances that will help you live complete for longer.

MAKES: 2 servings

PREPARATION TIME: 10 minutes

Calories in step with serving: 243

½ cup/120ml Filtered Water 1 cup/240ml Plain Yogurt

2½ cups/350g Chilled Papaya, peeled and chopped 2 teaspoons Fresh Ginger, grated

1 scoop Unsweetened Protein Powder

2 teaspoons Maple Syrup or desired sweetener (optional)

4 Ice Cubes

Directions

Add the water to a smoothie maker or blender. Add the final components and pulse till smooth.

Start drinking the smoothie into 2 glasses & serve immediately.

Mango Nilla Fudge

This is a splendidly cool and clean smoothie that of full of antioxidant-rich fruits and protein powder. This drink is guaranteed to satisfy your flavor buds!

MAKES: 2 servings

PREPARATION TIME: 10 minutes

Calories according to serving: 237

1 cup/240ml Milk

½ cup/120ml Plain Yogurt

½ cup/94g Mango Chunks, frozen 1 cup/145g Blueberries, frozen

1 scoop Unsweetened Protein Powder

½ teaspoon Vanilla Extract

4 Ice Cubes

Directions

Add the milk to a smoothie maker or blender. Add the closing elements and pulse until smooth.

Start drinking the smoothie into 2 glasses & serve immediately.

Chocolaty Almond Banza

Get energized with this amazingly smooth and yet scrumptious smoothie. This smoothie will be a incredible deal with for chocolate lovers.

MAKES: 2 servings

PREPARATION TIME: 10 minutes

Calories in step with serving: 356

2 cups/480ml Milk

2 big Bananas, peeled and sliced 2 tablespoons Cacao Powder

1 scoop Unsweetened Protein Powder

2 tablespoons Almond Meal

1 teaspoon Honey or desired sweetener (optional)

4 Ice Cubes

Directions

Add the milk to a smoothie maker or blender. Add the following ingredients & pulse it until smooth.

Start drinking the smoothie into 2 glasses & serve immediately.

Strawberry Chocolate Medal

This is one of the tastier and healthful smoothie recipes with white chocolate. This scrumptious smoothie will maintain you complete for a long time.

MAKES: 2 servings

PREPARATION TIME: 10 minutes

Calories in step with serving: 353

2 cups/480ml Milk

2 cups/288g Strawberries, frozen and hulled 1 small Banana, peeled and sliced

1 scoop Unsweetened Protein Powder 2 tablespoons White Chocolate Chips 2 tablespoons Chia Seeds

4 Ice Cubes

Directions

Add the milk to a smoothie maker or blender. Add the last substances and pulse till smooth.

Start drinking the smoothie into 2 glasses & serve immediately.

Pistachio Mango Cream

This recipe makes a first-rate tasting smoothie which has a healthful combo of elements. The pistachios used in this recipe upload a exceptional texture to this smoothie.

MAKES: 2 servings

PREPARATION TIME: 10 minutes

Calories in step with serving: 325

1 cup/240g Organic Coconut Water, unsweetened

1 teaspoon Fresh Lemon juice

¾ cup/180ml Plain Yogurt

2 cups/373g Mango Chunks, frozen

1 scoop Unsweetened Protein Powder

1 tablespoon unsalted Pistachios, chopped

1 teaspoon Honey or favored sweetener (optional)

¼ teaspoon Vanilla Extract

4 Ice Cubes

Directions

Add the coconut water to a smoothie maker or blender. Add the last ingredients and pulse till smooth.

Start drinking the smoothie into 2 glasses & serve immediately.

Blueberry Chia Delight

This recipe is a perfect mixture for a notable tasting smoothie. Everyone who tastes this smoothie may additionally find it irresistible and need more!

MAKES: 2 servings

PREPARATION TIME: 10 minutes

Calories consistent with serving: 319

2 cups/480ml Milk

1 cup/187g Mango Chunks, frozen 1 cup/145g Blueberries, frozen

1 scoop Unsweetened Protein Powder

2 tablespoons Chia Seeds

½ teaspoon Honey or desired sweetener (optional)

4 Ice Cubes

Directions

Add the milk to a smoothie maker or blender. Add the last elements and pulse until smooth.

Start drinking the smoothie into 2 glasses & serve immediately.

LOW SUGAR & DIABETIC SMOOTHIES
Kiwi Peach Sorbet

This refreshing smoothie has a delicious and mellow flavor of kiwi and peach. The combination with yogurt and milk makes this a lovely, creamy smoothie.

MAKES: 2 servings

PREPARATION TIME: 10 minutes

Calories in step with serving: 185

½ cup/120ml Fat-Free Milk

1 cup/240ml Fat-Free Plain Yogurt

1¼ cups/213g Peach, peeled, pitted and chopped 2 Kiwis, peeled and chopped

4 Ice Cubes

Directions

Add the milk to a smoothie maker or blender. Add the last substances and pulse until smooth.

Start drinking the smoothie into 2 glasses & serve immediately.

Dandelion Greens Shimmer

This wholesome and engaging smoothie, bursting with the taste of mixed berries, combines sparkling dandelion vegetables very nicely.

MAKES: 2 servings

PREPARATION TIME: 10 minutes

Calories consistent with serving: 165

1½ cups/360ml Unsweetened Almond Milk 2 cups/280g Mixed Berries, frozen

2 cups/110g Fresh Dandelion Greens 2 tablespoons Flaxseeds

4 Ice Cubes

Directions

Add the almond milk to a smoothie maker or blender. Add the last components and pulse until smooth.

Start drinking the smoothie into 2 glasses & serve immediately.

Strawberry Pixie

This recipe stands as one of nice mixtures for strawberry and rhubarb. This smoothie prepares a tangy and candy treat for warm summer season days.

MAKES: 2 servings

PREPARATION TIME: 10 minutes

Calories according to serving: 111

1½ cups/360ml Unsweetened Almond Milk

½ cup/120ml Fat-Free Plain Yogurt 1 cup/122g Rhubarb, chopped

1½ cups/216g Strawberries, frozen

½ teaspoon Vanilla Extract

four Ice Cubes

Directions

Add the almond milk to a smoothie maker or blender. Add the remaining substances and pulse until smooth.

Start drinking the smoothie into 2 glasses & serve immediately.

Apple Almond Pearl

This delightful apple smoothie has a wonderful texture from the addition of chopped almonds.

MAKES: 2 servings

PREPARATION TIME: 10 minutes

Calories consistent with serving: 374

1½ cups/360ml Unsweetened Almond Milk

½ cup/120ml Fat-Free Plain Yogurt

3 big Apples, peeled, cored and chopped

½ cup/48g Almonds, chopped

½ teaspoon Vanilla Extract Pinch of Ground Cinnamon

four Ice Cubes

Directions

Add the almond milk to a smoothie maker or blender. Add the remaining elements and pulse till smooth.

Start drinking the smoothie into 2 glasses & serve immediately.

Cranapple Green Pie

This smoothie is a terrific combination of herbal sweetness and tartness. The apple and cranberries splendidly compliment the clean greens in this recipe.

MAKES: 2 servings

PREPARATION TIME: 10 minutes

Calories in step with serving: 173

1½ cups/360ml Filtered Water

2 huge Apples, peeled, cored and chopped 1 cup/110g Cranberries, frozen

1 cup/144g Strawberries, peeled and sliced 2 cups/60g Fresh Mixed Greens

4 Ice Cubes

Directions

Add the water to a smoothie maker or blender. Add the ultimate components and pulse till smooth.

Start drinking the smoothie into 2 glasses & serve immediately.

Papaya Green Sauce

This is a healthy and scrumptious way to revel in a aggregate of papaya and vegetables. This smoothie is flavorful and nutritious, and it may be successful with all who flavor it.

MAKES: 2 servings

PREPARATION TIME: 10 minutes

Calories consistent with serving: 171

1½ cups/360ml Filtered Water

2 cups/280g Papaya, peeled and chopped 1 big Apple, peeled, cored and chopped 1 medium Cucumber, peeled and chopped

2 cups/110g Fresh Dandelion Greens, chopped 1 teaspoon Fresh Ginger, peeled and chopped

four Ice Cubes

Directions

Add the water to a smoothie maker or blender. Add the last components and pulse till smooth.

Start drinking the smoothie into 2 glasses & serve immediately.

Spinach Cherry Blossom

This is a totally easy and healthful smoothie recipe that makes a naturally sweetened drink despite the addition of spinach.

MAKES: 2 servings

PREPARATION TIME: 10 minutes

Calories per serving: 137

1½ cups/360ml Unsweetened Almond Milk 1 cup/180g Cherries, pitted and frozen

2 cups/60g Fresh Baby Spinach

½ teaspoon Vanilla Extract

four Ice Cubes

Directions

Add the almond milk to a smoothie maker or blender. Add the closing ingredients and pulse till smooth.

Start drinking the smoothie into 2 glasses & serve immediately.

Cantaloupe Swizzle

This is a cantaloupe smoothie that is without a doubt delicious. The addition of clean carrot juice adds a sincerely fresh taste to this smoothie.

MAKES: 2 servings

PREPARATION TIME: 10 minutes

Calories in line with serving: 171

½ cup/120ml Fresh Carrot juice 1 cup/240ml Fat-Free Plain Yogurt

2 cups/312g Ripe Cantaloupe, seeded, peeled and chopped 1 cup/123g Raspberries

4 Ice Cubes

Directions

Add the carrot juice to a smoothie maker or blender. Add the remaining ingredients and pulse till smooth.

Start drinking the smoothie into 2 glasses & serve immediately.

Gingery Peach Boogie

This smoothie is a fresh blast of peach with ginger. The addition of flaxseeds and vanilla extract provides a completely unique flavor to this drink.

MAKES: 2 servings

PREPARATION TIME: 10 minutes

Calories according to serving: 118

1 cup/240ml Fat-Free Milk 1 cup/240ml Filtered Water

1 huge Peach, peeled, pitted and chopped

½ teaspoon Fresh Ginger, chopped

2 tablespoons Flaxseeds

½ teaspoon Vanilla Extract

Directions

Add the milk and water to a smoothie maker or blender. Add the final substances and pulse till smooth.

Start drinking the smoothie into 2 glasses & serve immediately.

Blackberry Almond Cobbler

This is a satisfying and tasty smoothie. This deliciously flavored drink has an super source of brilliant meals nutrients that are all mixed with a slight vanilla taste.

MAKES: 2 servings

PREPARATION TIME: 10 minutes

Calories according to serving: 278

2 cups/480ml Unsweetened Almond Milk 3 cups/432g Blackberries, frozen

½ cup/48g Almonds, chopped

1 tablespoon Chia Seeds

½ teaspoon Vanilla Extract

Directions

Add the almond milk to a smoothie maker or blender. Add the remaining elements and pulse till smooth.

Start drinking the smoothie into 2 glasses & serve immediately.

Peachy Plum Ripple

This drink is a dietary powerhouse with a mixture of peach and plum. It is a slightly sweet and terrific pleasant smoothie.

MAKES: 2 servings

PREPARATION TIME: 10 minutes

Calories per serving: 117

1 cup/240ml Unsweetened Almond Milk

½ cup/120ml Fresh Strawberry juice

2 large Peaches, peeled, pitted and chopped 1 Plum, seeded, peeled and sliced

Pinch of Ground Cinnamon

four Ice Cubes

Directions

Add the almond milk to a smoothie maker or blender. Add the last substances and pulse until smooth.

Start drinking the smoothie into 2 glasses & serve immediately.

DAIRY-FREE SMOOTHIES

Banana Spinach Blast

This is a delicious smoothie made with banana, spinach and almond milk. This drink may be a perfect preference for a nutritional boost.

MAKES: 2 servings

PREPARATION TIME: 10 minutes

Calories in line with serving: 152

1¼ cups/300ml Unsweetened Almond Milk 2 Bananas, peeled, sliced and frozen

2 cups/60g Fresh Spinach, chopped 1 tablespoon Chia Seeds

1 teaspoon Vanilla Extract

4 Ice Cubes

Directions

Add the almond milk to a smoothie maker or blender. Add the remaining substances and pulse until smooth.

Start drinking the smoothie into 2 glasses & serve immediately.

Nutty Pumpkin Latte

This recipe makes a rich and creamy smoothie that tastes similar to a delectable pumpkin pie! The cashew nuts on this drink provide a creamy base to this smoothie.

MAKES: 2 servings

PREPARATION TIME: 10 minutes

Calories per serving: 344

1½ cups/360ml Soy Milk

¾ cup/180g Pumpkin Puree

1 huge Banana, peeled, sliced and frozen

¼ cup/34g Cashew nuts, chopped

2 tablespoons Maple Syrup or desired sweetener (optional) 1 teaspoon Pumpkin Pie Spice

4 Ice Cubes

Directions

Add the soy milk to a smoothie maker or blender. Add the following ingredients & pulse until smooth.

Start drinking the smoothie into 2 glasses & serve immediately.

Cranberry Coco Swoosh

This is a smoothie with a splendidly scrumptious tart flavor of cranberries. The sweetness of the banana and dates in this recipe perfectly suit the tartness of the cranberries.

MAKES: 2 servings

PREPARATION TIME: 10 minutes

Calories in line with serving: 491

1 cup/240 ml Unsweetened Coconut Milk 1 cup/240 ml Fresh Orange juice

1½ cups/a hundred sixty five g Fresh Cranberries

1 Large Banana, peeled, sliced and frozen

4 Dates, pitted and chopped (or preferred sweetener to taste)

1 teaspoon Vanilla Extract

Directions

Add the coconut milk and orange juice to a smoothie maker or blender. Add the closing substances and pulse till smooth.

Start drinking the smoothie into 2 glasses & serve immediately.

Creamy Mango Butter

This is a healthful and scrumptious recipe to that makes properly use of a candy mango.

The fresh lime juice in this smoothie gives a pleasant clean contact to the wonder of the mango.

MAKES: 2 servings

PREPARATION TIME: 10 minutes

Calories consistent with serving: 340

1¼ cups/300ml Filtered Water

2 tablespoons Fresh Lime juice

2 cups/373g Mango, peeled, pitted, chopped and frozen

¼ cup/66g Coconut Butter

1 tablespoon Maple Syrup or preferred sweetener (optional)

4 Ice Cubes

Directions

Add the water to a smoothie maker or blender. Add the remaining substances and pulse till smooth.

Start drinking the smoothie into 2 glasses & serve immediately.

Raspberry Beet Cluster

This is a colourful and fantastically colored smoothie with a blend of raspberries and beets. This smoothie is as healthy and scrumptious as it's far beautiful!

MAKES: 2 servings

PREPARATION TIME: 10 minutes

Calories in line with serving: 105

1½ cups/360ml Organic Coconut Water

2 tablespoons Fresh Lemon juice

1 medium Beet, trimmed, peeled and chopped 1½ cups/185g Raspberries, frozen

Honey or favored sweetener, to taste (optional)

4 Ice Cubes

Directions

Add the coconut water to a smoothie maker or blender. Add the final ingredients and pulse till smooth.

Start drinking the smoothie into 2 glasses & serve immediately.

Fruity Kale Cabana

This wholesome smoothie is a exquisite mixture of clean fruits with kale. You may experience it without or with ice cubes in keeping with your preference.

MAKES: 2 servings

PREPARATION TIME: 10 minutes

Calories in step with serving: 317

1½ cups/360ml Coconut Water

1 Pear, peeled, cored and chopped

1 cup/140g Papaya, peeled and chopped 1 Banana, peeled, sliced and frozen

2 cups/134g Fresh Kale, trimmed and chopped

2 tablespoons Almond Butter

1 tablespoon Honey or preferred sweetener to taste (optional)

4 Ice Cubes

Directions

Add the coconut water to a smoothie maker or blender. Add the ultimate components and pulse till smooth.

Start drinking the smoothie into 2 glasses & serve immediately.

Mixed Fruit Critters

This recipe is a delicious aggregate of three culmination with water kefir and chia seeds. This delicious fruity smoothie is dairy-loose and also healthful!

MAKES: 2 servings

PREPARATION TIME: 10 minutes

Calories in keeping with serving: 166

½ cup/120ml Coconut Milk Kefir

½ cup/120ml Filtered Water

1 cup/140g Cherries, pitted and frozen

2 cups/373g Mango, peeled, pitted, chopped and frozen

½ cup/70g Mixed Berries, Frozen

1 tablespoon Chia Seeds

Directions

Add the kefir to a smoothie maker or blender. Add the last substances and pulse till smooth.

Start drinking the smoothie into 2 glasses & serve immediately.

Creamy Orange Nirvana

This is an incredible recipe for a creamy smoothie which is a natural power booster! The aggregate of substances in this drink makes for a delicious and wholesome smoothie.

MAKES: 2 servings

PREPARATION TIME: 10 minutes

Calories in step with serving: 294

1½ cups/360ml Orange juice 1 cup/30g Fresh Spinach

1 small Avocado, peeled, pitted and chopped

½ teaspoon Fresh Ginger, finely chopped Pinch of Ground Cinnamon

4 Ice Cubes

Directions

Add the orange juice to a smoothie maker or blender. Add the ultimate substances and pulse until smooth.

Start drinking the smoothie into 2 glasses & serve immediately.

Minty Kiwi Gelato

This smoothie is not simplest a clean and funky drink; it is also a rich source of healthy nutrients. Sit returned and experience this exciting mixture of kiwi and honeydew melon each time of the day.

MAKES: 2 servings

PREPARATION TIME: 10 minutes

Calories in step with serving: 124

1½ cups/360ml Filtered Water

1 tablespoon Fresh Lime juice

1 cup/177g Kiwi, peeled and sliced

1 cup/156g Fresh Honeydew Melon, chopped

6 Fresh Mint Leaves

1 tablespoon Honey or favored sweetener (optional)

4 Ice Cubes

Directions

Add the water and lime juice to a smoothie maker or blender. Add the final elements and pulse till smooth.

Start drinking the smoothie into 2 glasses & serve immediately.

Zesty Peach Paradise

This is a smoothie packed with the proper flavors of peaches! Fresh lemon juice in this drink splendidly complements the peach flavors for optimum effect.

MAKES: 2 servings

PREPARATION TIME: 10 minutes

Calories in keeping with serving: 110

1¼ cups/300ml Unsweetened Almond Milk

1 tablespoon Fresh Lemon juice

2 massive Peaches, peeled, pitted and chopped

1 tablespoon Maple Syrup or favored sweetener (optional)

¼ teaspoon Vanilla Extract

four Ice Cubes

Directions

Add the almond milk and lemon juice to a smoothie maker or blender. Add the ultimate ingredients and pulse till smooth.

Start drinking the smoothie into 2 glasses & serve immediately.

HEALTHY KIDS SMOOTHIES
Peachy Pistachio Treat

This smoothie is a scrumptious combination of banana, peach yogurt and milk with a touch of pistachio. It makes a incredible drink which tastes like pistachio ice cream.

MAKES: 2 servings

PREPARATION TIME: five minutes

Calories per serving: 320

1 cup/240ml Milk

1 cup/240ml Peach Yogurt

2 medium Bananas, peeled and sliced three tablespoons Pistachio Nuts, chopped

4 Ice Cubes

Directions

Add the milk to a smoothie maker or blender. Add the final substances and pulse until smooth.

Start drinking the smoothie into 2 glasses & serve immediately.

Chocolaty Banana Swirl

This yummy chocolaty banana smoothie is a first rate manner for your children to start the day. This smoothie is guaranteed to come to be your kid's favourite drink.

MAKES: 2 servings

PREPARATION TIME: five minutes

Calories per serving: 342

1¼ cups/300ml Milk

2 big Frozen Bananas, peeled and sliced 1 teaspoon Vanilla Extract

2 tablespoons Dark Chocolate Chips

2 tablespoons Pecan Nuts

Directions

Add the milk to a smoothie maker or blender. Except for the chocolate chips, add the remaining components and pulse until smooth.

Add the chocolate chips and pulse till they're kind of chopped.

Start drinking the smoothie into 2 glasses & serve immediately.

Strawberry Banana Twist

This recipe makes a wonderfully delicious and fruity smoothie with a touch of chocolate flavor. Your infants will love to enjoy this smoothie!

MAKES: 2 servings

PREPARATION TIME: 5 minutes

Calories in line with serving: 218

1½ cups/360ml Milk

2 cups/288g Fresh Strawberries, hulled and sliced 1 big Frozen Banana, peeled and sliced

2 tablespoons Cacao Powder 1 teaspoon Vanilla Extract

four Ice Cubes

Directions

Add the milk to a smoothie maker or blender. Add the remaining substances and pulse until smooth.

Start drinking the smoothie into 2 glasses & serve immediately.

Spinach Banana Milano

This is a wholesome and electricity boosting smoothie, best for children. The almond butter gives this scrumptious smoothie a sweet creamy taste.

MAKES: 2 servings

PREPARATION TIME: five minutes

Calories consistent with serving: 301

1½ cups/360ml Milk

1 tablespoon Almond Butter

2 large Frozen Bananas, peeled and sliced 1½ cups/45g Fresh Baby Spinach

1 tablespoon Honey, or favored sweetener (optional)

Directions

Add the milk to a smoothie maker or blender. Add the ultimate components and pulse till smooth.

Start drinking the smoothie into 2 glasses & serve immediately.

Peachy Butter Berry

This recipe combines peach and blueberries to make a deliciously fruity smoothie. The addition of peanut butter in this drink adds a lovely peanut flavor.

MAKES: 2 servings

PREPARATION TIME: five minutes

Calories according to serving: 254

1½ cups/360ml Milk

1 cup/144g Blueberries, frozen

1 Fresh Peach, peeled, pitted and chopped

2 tablespoons Natural Peanut Butter

¼ teaspoon Vanilla Extract

Directions

Add the milk to a smoothie maker or blender. Add the ultimate components and pulse till smooth.

Start drinking the smoothie into 2 glasses & serve immediately.

Vanilla Almond Truffle

This recipe makes a healthful smoothie with a adorable nutty texture. The addition of dates to this drink brings a pleasant and natural sweetness.

MAKES: 2 servings

PREPARATION TIME: 10 minutes

Calories consistent with serving: 219

¼ cup/60ml Almond Milk 1 cup/240ml Vanilla Yogurt 2 Dates, pitted and chopped

1 teaspoon Vanilla Extract

2 tablespoons Almonds, chopped

4 Ice Cubes

Directions

Add the almond milk and yogurt to a smoothie maker or blender. Add the remaining components and pulse until smooth.

Start drinking the smoothie into 2 glasses & serve immediately.

Pineapple Cherry Craze

This recipe has a fantastic aggregate of fruit that makes for a excellent tasty smoothie. This scrumptious and citrus flavored smoothie is packed complete of wholesome vitamins.

MAKES: 2 servings

PREPARATION TIME: 10 minutes

Calories according to serving: 300

1 cup/240ml Fresh Orange juice

½ cup/120ml Plain Yogurt

1 cup/165g Pineapple Chunks, frozen 1 cup/165g Cherries, pitted and frozen 1 small Banana, peeled and sliced

½ tablespoon Chocolate Chips, overwhelmed

Directions

Add the orange juice and yogurt to a smoothie maker or blender. Except for the chocolate chips, add the last substances and pulse till smooth.

Start drinking the smoothie into 2 glasses & serve immediately

Top with the beaten chocolate chips and serve immediately.

Mixed Fruit Ripple

This is a colorful and scrumptious fruit smoothie. This smoothie will fulfill your kid's sweet tooth in a wholesome way.

MAKES: 2 servings

PREPARATION TIME: 10 minutes

Calories according to serving: 185

1 cup/240ml Fresh Orange juice

½ cup/120ml Fresh Cherry juice 1 Kiwi, peeled and chopped

1 cup/187g Mango Chunks

four Ice Cubes

1 tablespoon Shredded Coconut (optional)

Directions

Add the orange juice and cherry juice to a smoothie maker or blender. Add the ultimate ingredients, besides for the coconut, and pulse until smooth.

Start drinking the smoothie into 2 glasses & serve immediately., top with the coconut and serve immediately.

Vanilla Grape Jiggles

Enjoy this grape flavored smoothie that's enhanced with a pleasing vanilla flavor. It is antioxidant-rich and filled with healthy protein nutrition. You may additionally replacement grapes with your favorite berries to make this recipe even more interesting.

MAKES: 2 servings

PREPARATION TIME: 10 minutes

Calories per serving: 316

¾ cup/180ml Milk

1 cup/240ml Plain Yogurt

2 cups/184g Seedless Grapes, frozen

2 tablespoons Honey, or favored sweetener

½ teaspoon Vanilla Extract

Directions

Add the milk to a smoothie maker or blender. Add the final elements and pulse till smooth.

Start drinking the smoothie into 2 glasses & serve immediately.

Apple Pecan Pie

This recipe makes a thick and fruit smoothie full of banana, apple and pecans. Your children will love this healthful smoothie!

MAKES: 2 servings

PREPARATION TIME: 10 minutes

Calories in line with serving: 428

1½ cups/360ml Milk

2 Apples, peeled, cored and chopped 2 Bananas, peeled and sliced

1 tablespoon Honey, or preferred sweetener 2 tablespoons Pecan nuts, chopped

Directions

Add the milk to a smoothie maker or blender. Add the final components and pulse until smooth.

Start drinking the smoothie into 2 glasses & serve immediately.

LET'S FINISH STRONG!

I'm satisfied that you've joined me in making wholesome and attractive smoothies. As you continue, you could locate your self-getting greater innovative and making your own favorite combinations. In the end, you will obtain the nutritious advantages of mixing fresh fruits and vegetables. Each glass of those super food smoothies will bring you one step (perhaps even several steps) toward your aim to stay healthy, shed pounds and finish strong.

Now, you can revel in a first rate collection of flavorful smoothie recipes in your smoothie maker or blender. From breakfast smoothies to high strength smoothies, this e-book offers lots of clean ways to like smoothies any time of day. For a quick power raise, try any of the smoothies which might be combined with culmination and green vegetables. For rapid weight loss, try the weight reduction smoothies or another water primarily based smoothies. Remember that the purpose is to have amusing blending up your preferred smoothie elixir at the same time as also enhancing your health.

All in all, this e book is a vital smoothie maker companion with creative and pleasurable smoothie making ideas. Like me, you'll be beaming with power as you revel in restored health, stimulated cleansing and focused weight reduction. Enjoy the raise of wholefoods into every glass of smoothie.

Thanks again for choosing my Smoothie Maker Recipe Book. If you have determined it to be beneficial, I would respect if you will review my book on Amazon kindle store you don't know how we get benefit from me . Let's finish strong—the healthy way!

From my glass to yours,

Dr. Erick Mackarni

www.ingramcontent.com/pod-product-compliance
Lightning Source LLC
Chambersburg PA
CBHW081405130726
47998CB00011B/3079